An Aviary of Small Birds

Karen McCarthy Woolf was born in London to an English mother and a Jamaican father. She is the recipient of the Kate Betts Memorial Prize and an Arts and Humanities Research Council scholarship from Royal Holloway, where she is a PhD candidate. She is the editor of three literary anthologies, most recently *Ten: The New Wave* (Bloodaxe, 2014). Her poetry has appeared in publications including *Poetry Review*, *Prairie Schooner* and *Modern Poetry in Translation*.

KAREN McCARTHY WOOLF

An Aviary of Small Birds

Oxford*Poets*

CARCANET

First published in Great Britain in 2014 by
Carcanet Press Limited
Alliance House
Cross Street
Manchester M2 7AQ

www.carcanet.co.uk

A CIP catalogue record for this book is available from the British Library

ISBN 978 1 90618 814 6

The publisher acknowledges financial assistance from Arts Council England

Typeset by XL Publishing Services, Exmouth

For Otto McCarthy Woolf
7 August 2009

Contents

Acknowledgements

Thanks are due to the editors who first published the following poems: 'Morbleu', 'Mort-Dieu', 'Yellow Logic', 'White Butterflies', 'My Wings Beat Against the Glass' and 'The Weather in the Womb' in *Ten New Poets from Spread the Word* (Bloodaxe, 2010); 'Where Steel Clatters' in *Poetry London* (Spring, 2010); 'Wing' in *Poetry Review* (Winter, 2010); 'Harvest' in *The Rialto* (Autumn, 2011); 'Missing' in *Magma: 50*; 'Tasting Note for Grief #17' in *Poetry from Art* (Tate Modern, 2011); 'A Small Bird on a Tree of 12 Metres' in *Poetry Review* (Spring, 2012); 'The Paperwork' in *Poetry Wales* (Spring, 2012); 'Moon in Her Many Guises' was published in *Oxford Poets 2013*; 'July', 'Of August', 'Reasons to Fear Butterflies', 'I Remember Your Mother Dying', 'Of Roadkill and Other Corpses' in *Prairie Schooner* (Summer, 2014). 'The Wish' was a runner-up in the Cardiff International Poetry Competition in 2011. 'An Aviary of Small Birds' was one of the poems dropped in the Rain of Poems by Casagrande Collective at Poetry Parnassus, Southbank (London) 2012.

I would like to thank the following people and organisations for their support, advocacy and encouragement over the years: Arts Council England; Moniza Alvi; Paula Barder; Malika Booker; Ruth Borthwick and the Arvon Foundation; Bea Colley; David Constantine; Kwame Dawes; Bernardine Evaristo; Emma Hewett; Selima Hill; Mimi Khalvati, whose editorial guidance and teaching has been invaluable; Mum, Zoe, Lucy, Ricky; Pascale Petit, for all her creative inspiration at Tate Modern and beyond; all the librarians at the Poetry Library; the Poetry School; Spread the Word; Michael Symmons Roberts; Jo Shapcott; Nathalie Teitler and all the Complete Works Family; Simon Woolf.

The Undertaker

wears white gloves
and his left hand waves
on the crowd, moves

slowly as if under
the surface where water
swims sinuous as an elver

that darts between clouds
of ink in violet reeds
weightless as birds.

Wing

We find you, dear Wing,
in the half-dark
on the way back from the piglets,
your knuckle of raw bone
and streak of claw-white quills
torn from the socket.

A grey goose soars
up high where hot-air balloons drift
and the wind is a shape
to wrap yourself around
solid but unseen, a somersault
inside the womb;

here, folded to a cup of hands,
plump as a wood pigeon
in the long, flat January grass
you are singular and intense
like a girl breathing quietly by a window,
her just-cut hair pressed against the glass.

My Limbs Beat Against the Glass

I am trapped in a room where my baby dies
and when I try to fight my way out

a Victorian lepidopterist with walrus whiskers
skewers my solar plexus

and pins me to a felt-backed board,
so my limbs beat against the glass

like a moth battering a paper lantern,
as he tightens the frame to a vacuum.

Morbleu

—rushes and there's no more

a whirl of empty dresses—
        in this mudcracked room
             palm frond feathers
          helicopter
      downwards
shallow roots torn
      a broken bird
          song explodes
      on a frequency of earth and lime
               too high to hear

     —we haven't got—
    a heart   beat

     —haven't got five minutes
a groan of sea
       shushes up on shore

     —rushes and there's no—
no *ha ha ha* of music
           and radio
     the thud of workmen
        clatter of hollow poles—scaffolding
a truck in first gear
        footsteps
        school

an O of bells clang-
       clangs across the river

    and then the hush
         of marble
     eyes unseen eyes unopened
            endlessly eyes

Mort-Dieu

Our son
dear God
is dead
and gone.
His tomb
was red
with blood
and warm
as tears.
He was
born still.
Was this
dear God
your will?

White Butterflies

Three white butterflies
flutter then land
on the artichoke spikes
in the walled garden.

White sky against the ash.
The wind in the leaves
a rush of sighs.

White lavender
at the edge of the pool.
White hydrangeas
wilted in the bouquet.
White lilies sticky with scent.
White tissues in the box.
White linen on the bed.
White curtains shrunk in the wash.
White muslin squares.
Your tiny white vests, unworn.

Yellow Logic

Was it because I should have
bought those handmade, pony-hair boots
that swung round my ankles like a mane?
I can't forget Spaghetti Beach
and the gypsy girl with a nose ring
who sold me a rotting shoulder bag
then cursed me.
    Perhaps, my darling boy, we'll meet
at the *piscina municipal* in Guadalest,
the one cut into the cliff,
surrounded by thick-bladed grass
green as Astroturf. I'll be lithe and sleek
as I back-flip into the water and pretend
I'm not afraid you'll disappear
like the sun on a so-so afternoon.

Missing

Every day I wake up and remember
your future is missing
and even though it never belonged to me

I take to the tow-paths of Amsterdam:
Herengracht, Singel... pin A5 posters
to vitiligoed tree trunks.

In the photo your eyes are closed
and you don't look like anything any more
but *you never know.*

So I scour the alleys, pause outside a school.
Is that you strapped to a stranger's chest,
the one in the blue-for-boy sling?

The Paperwork

I sit up in bed, try to make up my mind.
Will it change anything if I decide
your heart, liver, lungs, kidneys
are returned to the abdominal cavity?
My forefinger traces a path through
Option 5c: I understand these parts
will not be returned to their original position.

Your navel has not yet shrivelled,
each toenail is sacred.
Under *Other requests or concerns:*
hands, feet, face, hair—all must be left intact.
Brain to be restored to head, skin
stitched neatly and correctly.

I peer at the page on the doctor's lap.
Yes, they may saw through your breastbone,
but they'll sew your little tummy up
as if you were a rare mediaeval tapestry.
I'll make sure of that. *Eyes not to be touched.*
The doctor bites her lip, writes it in the box.

The Museum of Best Laid Plans
(fragment)

Exhibit 17c (ii). Early 21st-century commonly adapted
bedside cabinet—IKEA, Billy shelving in beech veneer
containing a collection of miscellaneous domestic trinkets
and various homeopathic medicines (possibly placebos).
From bottom up: one transparent plastic watch (stopped);
Dr Bach Rescue Remedy (30 ml dropper); calendula
thiossinaminum (6°), arnica, aconite; several paperback
books including a number of Pago-Christian *materia medica*
including *Sister Karol's Book of Spells and Blessings*;
Back to Eden; *African Holistic Health*; *The Fastest*
Way to Get Pregnant Naturally; and *Sonata Mulattica*
(poems). Shelves IV & V: containing 13 pairs of sunglasses
(designer and high-street) ranging from imitation tortoiseshell
(origin Lagos, Nigeria: c.1974) to 1950s bubblegum
pink rhinestone-studded (cf. early celebrity cultures partic.
An Audience with Dame Edna, 1986). Two boxes: above—
ProJuven (1.5 & 3%) (empty) with folded instructions
Applicare 1–2 misure di crema ogni giorno sulla zona
interna della braccia... below—A4 stationery (Conqueror)
W Uden & Sons Ltd, Funeral Directors, labelled Infant:
Locks of Hair.

The Registrar's Office

isn't really an office it's a cupboard with
no source of natural light, and I don't
realise it but I'm loved up like the other
mothers gazing at meconium as if it's fresh tar
on a road not an odourless, black shit
that's been on the boil for nine months and
Lydia, that's the registrar's name, she
gives me a paper cone of iced water from
the dispenser to calm me down and it
does calm me, the water flows through
me and now we're holding each other while
Simon's down in the mortuary and I tell
her all about how he lost his mother from
a brain tumour when I was six months
gone, how her name was Lydia too, that
it was so quick and now this.
We're still holding on when he comes back
then joins us in a circle of three and even
another form to fill in can't sober me up
as the morphine unpeels another mezzanine
of hell in a shopping centre where women
with rigid quiffs and rouged cheeks glide
up and down glass escalators and
people believe in the faux marble fountains
although it's all really a shimmering
colon. Anyway, I'm determined, I say,
as I leave the room, when I get out of here, if
it's the last thing I do, I *will* get you
a window because that's not right, expecting
someone to live and work and sign
death certificates without a window, no-one
should have to put up with that, it's not
right, she's a good person with
a good heart, she should have a window.

Of August

Two agents, an editor and a couple of publishers come to the University for a panel discussion. Going home on the train afterwards, one of the students writes a synopsis of the novel she plans to pitch to them at a later date: the story of a woman, The Protagonist, who, after many years of trying to conceive, is finally pregnant. Her Best Friend is bipolar and has just been diagnosed with inoperable cancer, aged 36.

The pregnancy is going well but The Protagonist is disconcerted to learn that her friend has decided to refuse conventional treatment in favour of acupuncture and classical Chinese medicine. Although The Protagonist is not against natural healthcare, equally she is unconvinced that acupuncture is the right choice: yes, The Best Friend has travelled widely in China and speaks and writes Mandarin, but she is not Chinese.

The baby is due that summer, in late July, or August—when both The Protagonist and The Best Friend share their birthdays. August is their favourite month and in late July, when the contractions begin, there is a moment when both friends worry the baby might be born too soon.

Unfortunately, the birth does not go as expected and the baby dies during a long labour on the 7th of August, two days after The Best Friend's birthday. There is evidence to suggest the hospital is at fault, although the consultant who goes over the autopsy results with The Protagonist and her partner advises them to concentrate on rebuilding their lives. He also tells them about his 18-year-old daughter who was killed in a car accident two weeks before she was due to take up a place at Oxford.

Time passes and The Best Friend decides to go scuba diving in Borneo. She is away for three months. When she returns she has lost a lot of weight and The Protagonist has a strong feeling it is too late. The Protagonist rings Another Friend and they try to devise a Strategy. But The Best Friend makes it very clear she does not want anyone in her life who does not support her treatment choice; right now she is focusing on feng shui and getting a new kitchen and bathroom fitted.

The Protagonist also has other things to focus on and the relationship falters under the strain. The Best Friend maintains a constantly shifting hierarchy that elicits an undertow of competition among all the female friends. This is confirmed when Another Another Friend rings and tells The Protagonist that The Best Friend has new test results that The Protagonist did not know about.

From this point on The Best Friend's medical situation intensifies and now the priority is pain and symptom management. The Best Friend would like to be more sociable but there is too much pain and her time is spent writhing on the sofa. Occasionally she is well enough to receive visitors or drink rosebud tea in the garden.

The kitchen and bathroom works continue, but The Best Friend is mugged on her way back from the building society with £2000 cash to pay the builder. The Protagonist says this is awful at the best of times and that these are not the best of times, but the Best Friend does not like this and refuses to return The Protagonist's calls for nearly a month.

The Best Friend has long, lustrous red hair and The Protagonist thinks this may be one of the reasons why she is resisting chemotherapy, but doesn't know how to broach this subject with The Best Friend.

Now it is summer again and The Best Friend is in and out of hospital. The last time The Protagonist sees The Best Friend she has to help her mother pin her to a bed with white metal bars that make it look like an oversized cot. The Best Friend is in a partial coma and cannot formulate words easily, but she rattles on the bars and asks The Protagonist to help her get out of this place, it's the hospital that's killing her.

Two days later The Best Friend dies in the hospital. It is the same hospital where The Protagonist's baby died, but in a different ward, without a view of the river. The Best Friend dies on the 5th of August, on her 38th birthday. The Protagonist is proud that her friend has managed to die on this day, because she knows it will have meant a lot, because it is her birthday, and it is August, and these things were important to her.

Pinhole Camera

Light accumulates slowly
inside her and the dead say
keep your chin up, look to the sky,

we can help you then.
Gradually a landscape appears
on photographic paper:

a brown river through glass,
white tourist boats that toot as they pass
a Chesterfield sofa carved in sand

where two black dogs
snap at each other's tails. A long
exposure that drags on

for years: giraffe necks in the zoo
as seen from the cycle path,
that stiff fox outside the timber yard—

its brush fascinating and erect;
at every other bus stop a boy with curly hair
or an infant held close to the breast.

Portrait of a Small Bird on a Tree of 12 Metres

after Giuseppe Penone

I

Inside where it is dark, where branches
criss cross—a tree stripped

and whittled, where the wood is denser
and leaves flicker like bonfires

lit at the end of summer, here
in the heart of the wood you are the light

not the shadow, an unsolved equation
in a dog-eared exercise book.

II

Cross the red line and
the room changes size, dimension

—the ceiling reaches for a lightning spear,
wreaks havoc on a rectangle

of artificial daybreak while a rusted girder
snaps at a toddler on the bus—

everything I want is up there, just
out of reach, in the white emulsion.

Of Jealousy

I will not say much about the etymology but it is connected to zealous. There is a similar link between grammar and glamour. Thinking again of envy, the verb is *envier* in French whereas in Spanish *enviar* means to send. Perhaps this active element is why envy has Sin status while jealousy does not. I am envious of other people's ability to concentrate and the gulls I can see from the window.

I am reminded of the beach in Sitges, when a bird, possibly a small parakeet, was flying amongst the sunbathers. The bird kept launching itself at the waves and a man (middle-aged, fully clothed, quite fat) was trying to catch it. Although it looked like the bird might drown, the man's outstretched hands seemed sinister. The bird fluttered towards the sea, the man waded out another inch in rolled-up trousers. This continued for some time. Then I saw another man dragging a Persian cat down the boardwalk on a lead.

I Remember Your Mother Dying

after Craig Raine

I remember
  We were driving, it was a weekday, we stopped at a motorway service station just outside Bristol, although of course it could have been in any of those deadening, uniform places which always make me think of how a tree has no choice as to where it grows, the seed falls as the wind takes it or saplings are planted in military rows. We were queuing for herbal tea: I was four months pregnant and watching what I ate.

I remember
  Your father on the phone, with the news, you reaching for your wallet, the tea hot on my tongue as I sucked it through the little slit in the white plastic cup cover.

I remember
  Your mother, how she always came to the yellow front door to greet us, often in an apron, as we drove up the track to the house, squashed into the front seat of your father's Land Rover. How she always smiled brightly and waved even though she never smiled for photos, barely even on her wedding day. How she baked bread and grew vegetables in the polytunnel and the walled kitchen garden: an espaliered peach, artichokes and figs. How you said your childhood was perfect.

I remember
  The funeral. The eulogy I wrote. I watched your father as he vetted the text, how he paused when he reached the part where I said I knew her spirit would live on, exhaled when I qualified it with 'in the house and garden'. The only correction he required was for me to change glacé cherries to maraschino.

I remember
  The service was in a modern crematorium with a large stained glass window that looked out onto a hillside. There was something about the aspect, the slope into the horizon. Two

things happened and I can't remember the order in which they occurred. A car alarm kept on sounding while the Bach Choir was singing. This would have been intrusive at any service, but your mother hated loudness and despised cars. Eventually it abated then started again, before finally stopping. The second thing that happened was a hawk flew in an arc right across the diagonal of the window. Many people in the room noticed it and seemed pleased, relieved even, that something beautiful had taken place.

I remember
Your brother, a mathematician, how he sat with your mother and wrote a list of all the places she wanted to visit. How we went to the gardens at Antony that were full of rhododendrons and camellias. Your brother took a lot of photographs of your mother and then I took the camera and tried to capture the three of you on a stone bench near the river, but your mother hid her face under her pale blue hood. I remember how, when she walked, your mother thrust out her chin and hopped down unaided from a wall overhanging the path. That night, when we got home, she went to bed and didn't get up again.

I remember
The first inkling had been at Christmas when she burnt the roast potatoes.

I remember
Her sitting in bed with her long white hair plaited and patting my stomach, telling me to make sure I took care of the baby. Her asking what we wanted and I mentioned the tall-backed farmhouse chair, how her eyes half closed in assent.

I remember
Trying to squash all the pills into the dispenser we'd bought with the days of the week embossed on them, but there were too many pills and a simpler system with a notebook was adopted instead. The mattress your father dragged into the bedroom so he could sleep at the foot of her hospital bed. How your mother liked to watch the birds at the feeder he had erected outside her window.

I remember
Her trying to remember certain words, reaching for them as if they were apples on a high bough.

I remember
How in the beginning she'd tried to hold on, as you held on to the idea she might survive until the baby was born for as long as you could. How in the last few days she kept murmuring the word oblivion.

Where Steel Clatters

A circular saw whines, the clouds are asphyxiated
blue, the sign to the sanatorium's dented
with bullet holes. A patch of shrunken gourds
accounts for the man in the pick-up truck.
A trail of corn seed, some sprouted with ears...

I need to know if it leads to a house
with boiled-sweet window-panes and a hag.
Another question: does the *Institut Pneumologie*
have anything to do with tyres? For now though,
just a foot-trudge over stones that turn

into boulders that rise and sink like lungs.
The woods have gobbled the sun
and in a clearing—there!—a burnt-out Renault.
Does it just feel like somebody's watching
or is somebody watching?

And I worry about the quiet, the dark, the map;
stick close behind you—just in case—even though
I know now, the worst things happen in brash,
fluorescent rooms where steel clatters
and silence is the total absence of movement.

Starlight

She wants to be as far away
from the gurney

and the empty metal cot
as starlight.

She wants a spinal anaesthetic
to flatten her like an iron,

so it's easy to forget
the way they failed

to electrocute life back.
But the birth

is close as the white spots
under her eyelids

when she stares into the sun
hoping to be blinded.

Fragments

i)
Your body is a splinter of star,
naked and unused, crash landed where steam
rises from the fens.

ii)
The lily stamen
bares its sticky fangs
        on this sweet nine-acre farm.

iii)
On Boxing Day we walk along the cliffs to Rame.
The wind a stream
        tunnelling through my fears.

iv)
All our small talk is meant.
How else can we smother this rage?

The Scales

and here that brainless spider in the sink
the one you try so hard to save
but end up killing
all the same.

Here the blood-stained pliers,
the two dark towers of buffalo skulls,
a brisk trade
in little girls' vaginas

Moon in Her Many Guises

SNOW

Her word is an ocean
of almond blossom
blown in under the door
by gales that
    bang shutters
against plastered walls.

ICE

Unexploited frozen reservoirs are
concealed under a polar nipple that
burns with pinpricks.

A probe is programmed to crash
into a shadowed crater in accordance with
The Outer Space Treaty.

There's water here, more than we've left
in the Sahara. If only it would melt.

Silver, sulphur, mercury and methane
are also unexpectedly unearthed
and now there's scope for future colonies.

Viewed from the observation platform
her solidified lakes shine like duck eggs.

WINTER

All her seas run dry
     and marrow dark;

though the Sea of Crises
overflows
     month after month.

CROW

And so the story goes…
white birds with black blood
cast shadows as they
touch down at Mumbai Airport
while Crow flies low
over baggage reclaim—
He drops a molten marble into the sky,
      gets the ball rolling…

EGG

An avocado stone
is planted, watered, watched
until its roots touch
the edge of the pot,
its cool clay belly.

Moon wants all the eggs
to synchronise
with the swell and fall
of moods, subtle
as the tides she charms
then spurns
as she elongates
the globe
into a watery
ovoid.

HARE

Rabbit kits grow commensurate
with her wane and wax

while the leveret embryo
is more Lenten:

it takes approximately 40 days
for a litter to emerge, fully furred,

from the capsule of the womb,
eyes already open.

The does are her familiars.
In the mating season

they rear up
and box with the bucks,

the last left standing mounts.
We see one flash into the woods

on the hill behind the house—
mistake it for a deer.

Her ears are everywhere:
the motorway's waterfall of noise

floods the morning, a train shrieks
at a teenage copse whose saplings

rush to their rooms and slam doors
over the crackle of fickle pylons,

another SMS pulses, thrushes
and finches pipe louder…

Did you know soft pellets are nibbled
direct from the anus?

No nourishment is wasted.
The digestive tract is calibrated finely.

Always alert, she knows
how to lie low, stomach pressed

to ridges of churned soil.
Trap her and she'll kick hard enough

to break her own back.
The only way for her to live is wild.

WOLF

Turmeric-eyed and luminous,
el día lunes, Monday too,
lupine, la lune, la una and
alone.
      She is never alone.

NECTAR

She's a perfect circle, her face round
as a pill stamped with the contours
of a dove who flies through a recurring dream
she had in the last days of the twentieth century,
where her non-existent lover flounders
in the prickly basalt of the Marsh of Sleep.
He wants her to fish him out, fling him
to her obedient groves where oranges cluster
like fledgling planets around the base
of tree trunks and honeysuckle garlands his curls
with trumpet flowers sweet as jam on a cracker.
But first you've got to come up to the castle,
make a move or two on the dance floor,
feel the bass thump as you trampoline
to yet another daybreak where blacked-up
Morris men sport pheasant feathers
in sawn-off top hats, clash sticks, knock wood
and suddenly the sky's a swimming pool
so you sink a fizzy gin at 9 a.m. in shades
that dull the dazzle she only reflects, let's not
forget and now you know what love is.

DOG

It is the time when all things ripen:
corn swells to teeth in the husk,
rivers pant in summer's heat
and the little streams are exhausted.

Who says your death is blameless?
I want to slip this August moon in a sack
and watch her wriggle like a puppy
as she's swallowed by the lake.

HARVEST

Even a star
     must share
          the sky with the Earth.

The horizon belongs to neither west nor east.

Nothing seems to sate
     us; we scramble arse
                  over tit & hate
to save
anything we can have.

If tears
were prayed-for rain we'd still starve.

THUNDER

Prophecies adorn the bedside table:
an orb of black roses, their scent metallic
as the clash of swords and shields
when the lights flicker in the museum's long,
glassy corridors as totems topple
and display cabinets splinter with fright.

On the bench in the hospital garden
endorphins invade my arteries
as microscopic pearls, involuntarily
suckled from a celestial breast.
A nurse doses me
with a hormone to plug my milk ducts.

BLUE

The clown has a power that comes from the thunder beings, not
from the animals or the earth. Being a clown gives you honour
but also shame. It brings you power, but you have to pay for it.

Lame Deer

Le Général keeps a silver shovel
in a Persian carpet bag; loves

a bad-boy rumble
down the hill in hot-rod prams.

His men pull old accordions out of hats,
an icy christening cake is smashed

in scars and face, an elbow in my soup
Sir! Bonnets big and white as parachutes.

Hankies flap like elephant ears, bare
cheeks rouged, tattooed with tear-

drops. A cavalry of spoons on knees,
bouncy bedsprings, laceless shoes.

How to cheer our Lady up they ask?
Face the firing squad. It's die or laugh.

Initiation's a crawl through fire.
Two years ago a mutt was boiled alive.

If soothing lullaby or harp don't work
then lightning quick like sharks

they make their move and strike;
advantage is their art's surprise.

What poxy dose of mathematics!
Every now and then she gets like this.

47

BLOOD

Death is out hunting tonight,
    the moon a torch in his hand.

Deer, bears, boar, babies…
    Sugar skulls and swaddled

loaves are offered up for *los angelitos*
    while songbirds dart, pick strands

of flesh from between his teeth
    their music constant as he strides.

Of course it doesn't really go like this:
    the doctor wastes

twenty minutes trying to scrape
    a sample from your scalp.

By the time they slice me open
    it's too late.

Blood-splashed aprons
    are binned with pointless sharps.

…Yet still, my love, I long for you,
    as the two caged canaries

who hop and whirr from the plastic perch
    to the nest coiled from wire

and filled with unfertilised eggs
    long for the ravine.

The Puppies

Come out and you get things.
The puppies are small.
Two fit in one hand like tennis balls.
The man in the bar, he has a hat.
Cinco semanas solo tienen.
One black, a little sleep in his eye.
The other brown, mottled
like a feather duster.
He says he's going to sell them,
all warm wet tongues and snuffle.

I know I said, my love, I would
free you from this grief, but it flows
through my body like blood. They eat
blood in this region. Boil it in vats
and spice it with pimento and bay.
Chicken blood or pig's. Not cow.
Then they pour it into white Tupperware
boxes and leave it to set into jelly.

The Iris Field

Waist deep in a sea of bearded
irises fragrant as old wine:
chocolate scented, Horizon Blue
we watch a partridge herd her brood
of nestlings in between the beds.
There must be fifteen little chicks.
We've no idea if they're Red Legged
or English Greys, until we look it up
in the *Big Book of British Birds*.
All eggs have a yolk that rises
up to the warmth of the hen's breast.
The chicks scatter as our shadows loom.
I want to hold one so *tightly*.

A Small Ball of Mercury

She is sensitive to heat
and cold in equal measure.
This girl never sits still.
Her thoughts are an electric
sea, turbulent
but calmed by watermelon
boats with paper sails.
She rises with the sun
and always wears
her thin glass straitjacket.
Wikipedia reports
the highest eccentricity
of orbit and she does fly close.
Neither one thing nor
the other, her message
is delivered under the cover
of moonlight.
She has no satellites
and if left to her own devices
dissipates, quickly.

Circle

—it's like a fish I can't catch
or a bird, there's a river I don't dare
dive into because of the currents—
but then I remember that time in the Cam
upstream by Grantchester Meadows
when two of us slipped underwater
from the side of the punt—the water's
cleaner, no pesticide run-offs—and I swam
breast-stroke alongside the boat, the thought
of getting out thick with the shudder of
unwanted silt sliding between my toes,
even there, where the water was so
undisturbed, as I think of this now, I lose
the original thread; I want to say the word
angular, as an answer to a question
I've never worked out, how the needle's
groove scores a blues in my head, the way
I can't stop it, worrying its path
into my consciousness, blaring away
from a bindweed flower speaker, scratchy
as a cat's claw and when I leave the house,
I may have to check whether the breeze
is a memory, cooling my ankles, you see
there's no virtue in bringing things
back round to the beginning, as my jaw
stiffens, as I grind my teeth.

Emotions

We can't omit
them. Tone
of voice is a stone
in motion.

The moon's
a mint–
white note
to self.
　　Mine
weigh a ton
most
of the time.

July

& today is
crackle planted inside me
        a pylon straddling
the borders of a field

& when there was no
anxiety
        in the full bloom of summer
when the pavements were dusty
        as my stomach swelled then dropped
I accentuated its taut lollipop by
        layering fuchsia and peony
conducting telegraphed conversations
        with my idea of you, mornings
I woke when the light was tentative
        scrutinised the gaps in the tree tops
and made videos of my feet
        breathless from weight pressing
on the diaphragm, a pillow squeezed
        between my thighs, a swooshing
water bomb and all of this
        not forgotten, as drifts of birdsong
black bullocks—stirks, jostling
        by the gate, berries just turning
from green to red, deep mud under hooves

Bamboo

—yes, the willow in the pot
from a friend who died young
wavers in the breeze

a crow preens
on the uppermost branch
of the ash

a green husk
lies abandoned on the pink
concrete terrace

the crow is silent
from the south west the sound
of a train passing

now the crow caws
three times making me jump
little birds flit

from branch to branch
on the buddleia
picking insects from its creases

the sun is still in the east
there's a chill
in the air, the bamboo wind chime

sounds its tone, like a tongue
clicking for a horse
a door closes

August

What will come to pass will pass.
On the seventh day of the eight month
the child will be born.

She waved Indian basil oil
under my nose and it really did bring the labour on
in that room with a large blue ball
and a view out to Big Ben.

I treated her like a maidservant
whose job it was to wring and wring towels,
she in a velvet dress and a wimple.

Of Roadkill and Other Corpses

After the birth she spends a year and a half taking photographs of dead animals and prizes the most pristine. Her collection includes a mole, its pink, fleshy digits spread wide like oars; an open-eyed fieldmouse with a blade of grass and a bluebottle on its flank; a hawk in a stream; a fledgling wren; a flattened rabbit in threshed straw, its hind legs splayed like an X in a crossword square; a field littered with disintegrating geese, their ribs and feathers matted to form a hardened, gelatinous web. There is also a radiant mallard surrounded by a constellation of dandelion flowers and clocks and finally, a pony on its back at the side of the road that cuts through Dartmoor. The pony's legs stick up into the air and a cylinder of dung protrudes halfway out of its anus below the arch of its tail. The pony's genitalia are exposed and she can be identified as a mare.

Against the Clock

It was never supposed to be like this.
Late arrival blows through her as a gale
rushing the corridors of a shabby hotel
where notices about the ethics
of towel laundering fail to convince
and catching the ferry is a prayer answered
while the task in hand blossoms
into an overblown saga of childlessness
and familial lack that clings
like cigarette smoke to her clothes.
Oh, how she longs for the luxury of thanks!

Otto

O my translucent bell
the best I can do is to sit
on the purple bench
under the Virginia creeper
and listen to the bamboo

wind chimes that sound
nothing like but remind
me of the sea: a keepsake
from another life, gentle
and full of careful planning.

Next to you I'm a swamp
with tender corners that suck
and sink. Day and night
the undergrowth simmers
as I try to avert my eyes

from its glitter—a crushed
Marlboro packet shines
like a fly agaric. Rickety
smoke rises from the surface
of the cello pool. And still

I think your voice can't reach
me, or worse you're saying
nothing, as I continue
my catastrophic rattle, your silence
constant as the roar of traffic.

Reasons to Fear Butterflies

Unexpected movement—
a suddenness

where nothing is as it seems, wings
dotted with owl eyes, ears
on furry tips

How they feed on our secretions:
sweat, saliva, tears

I imagine them
on the water's surface, sucking
the sea as if it were a teat

hours slashing the air
like blindness. Their silk a thread of fear
that runs from throat to clitoris

tingling

The Calf

The boat's engine fails
three times then starts.

Here, on this mass
of volcanic rock

the islanders say
the animal you need

always comes to you.
Off the coast of La Gomera

it's against the law
to swim with pilot whales

or other dolphins.
I want to be in the water

where the sea tugs
at my hair and the cry

of a blue and shiny calf
dozing on the surface,

guarded by 50-year-old aunts,
is a tone so high and long

it glows. All around
a communal whale brain

pulses. The little boat bobs
and then he's gone

down into the dark.
Something is better than nothing,

they tell you that.
This was not the sound

I'd waited for, but it was
as close as we'd ever got.

The Sooty Shearwaters

I can't remember the word
but think it'll make a difference if
I write it in Spanish—*pardella*
is the name you're looking for—
a small brown gull who heads
out to sea at dawn, in competition with
the dwindling pods of whales,
on the hunt for shoals of little fish
to swallow and regurgitate.

At night TVs and streetlamps
are switched off so the birds
can navigate by starlight
to find their young, nestled
in the crevices of cut-glass cliffs
that ricochet their calls.
Their cry is a sound so unique
visiting DJs sample it—a frequency
that works a bit like, but is not, sonar.

Hawk

I am most interested in the claws
and feet which are surprisingly municipal
in colour, like double yellow lines,

while the talons are brown as earwigs.
That's not to say the mottled feathers flowing
or that gurgle rushing over the corpse

so it disintegrates—the eye's already white—
isn't calming, because it *is* a comfort,
this return to water, to the stream, to the earth;

the mindless torrent of the brook,
gentle but insistent as it passes
under the broken gate piebald with moss.

Letter to Miriam

Forsythia buds nudge their way through snow
that betrays its promise to make everything
unknowable and melts. I think of you
and rue de la Croix d'Or, Van Gogh's chair
and other yellowness: pollen and bee stripes,
sherbet lemons and egg yolks, 40-watt bulbs.
Right now I have an urge to go swimming
at the Oasis where genies of steam rise
from the warm water. My thoughts are scattered:
what of the other life where I skin buffalo
and snore by the campfire? Who holds my son
now that his feet have been cast? Why here?
When more than a billion birds spiral out of the sky
each year, why don't we see them fall?

A Matter of Gravity

I think of the word nadir, how once
a boyfriend called Nader told me
his name meant river. I learnt
the word nadir from a girl called
Leila Nadir who had thick black hair:
you know she said *the opposite of zenith.*
Zenith also means path, through the sky
not the ground. The river is a tongue,
its flow an etymology, reaching
back to a damp source, but like language
the river stretches towards a new place,
a new identity, although, thinking
about it, no, the river seeks to *lose*
its identity, craves an anonymous
existence. *All the rivers run into the sea;*
yet the sea is not full. And what of
those rivers that never quite cut their way
through? Cut is the wrong verb, rivers
press, insinuate, overwhelm, insist, endure,
burrow; their flow supple as thought.
And I think of all those rivers rushing
towards namelessness, thundering on
to the coast, always with weight behind them.

The Last Sardine

And now we're hungry, it's time to eat
and we don't want shadows, sticks

and grass—we'd rather briny bacalao
or ling, some lumpfish caviar, perhaps

a hundred thousand tons of anchovies
an hour will keep us ticking over

until lunch, give us something salty
on the tongue, a squillion tiny pearls of roe,

a fin, a beak, some sacs of ink,
and when that's done we'll roast the gulls.

Swim Often

Swim often, the sea absorbs: this is my
advice to visitors on tiny islands
in the Atlantic who are feeling claustrophobic
and it's true, the water cradles me, I could die
with my head in her lap dreaming
of the time when I swim out beyond the buoys
where it gets choppy and the waves lick
my lips like an over-excited Irish wolfhound
and I look back at the shore and realise
the peninsula I was aiming for is further
than the jagged cliff studded with gorse and
blackberry bushes so I'll have to doggy
paddle home but it never crosses my mind
that I won't make it even as the tide turns;
I know I can swim that far—it'll just be harder—
yes, that's how I thought it would be
once I went under the knife and they stitched
me up with a needle curved like a crescent moon,
I thought *I've come this far* and waking up
to the sound of your voice was as certain
as the proliferation of Spanish bluebells
that screwdriver their way through the mossy lawn
when another April comes around; these are
the thoughts that surface, in the morning
in the shower, as my brain whirrs.   .

After August

At home in the garden
the unidentified shrub, tall
as a young tree, is dying,

its blackened leaves
and last year's flower clusters
shrivelled on structural branches.

I plan to cut back hard but fear
the reality of a hole
in the air. First the viburnum,

then the rose, now this:
black spot spreading and
I don't know how to root it out.

The sun blazes
on the school playground
where I splay unwanted shoes, clothes

and books on a bedspread.
A woman knocks us
down to two pounds for

the push-button phone,
but each of her three daughters
refuses the offer of a free book.

I'm sick of grief
and the disappointment summer exacts.
Maybe every plant is like a child

who can't imagine death,
as blossom is innocent
of the sacrifice it makes for fruit.

The Weather in the Womb

Autumn is head down in the sink.
The trees taste iron and wren
        droppings.
Oh my rustic plectrum!
Your music is
        where the leaf falls.

Where it falls
the river hums like a PC.

        Take note
of the ice on the water trough in the yard
and the Eskimo oil from deep sea fish
        caught by a bear
whose coat is a lichen of silver-tipped hair
fuzzy as alkanet.

There is a God
        and he dwells in the perfect
horse dung on the bridle path.

Evening is the hardest skin we carry.

As an Axe Misses the Tree

As an axe misses the tree
and a branch misses the bird,
as the ocean misses a sea
and a poem misses the word.

As a wave misses the moon
and purple misses blue,
as a song misses the tune
and a question misses who?

As a month misses the week
and a bulb misses the lamp,
as a skylight misses the street
and speakers miss the amp.

As a scratch misses the itch
and a plaster misses thumbs,
as a candle misses the wick
and Earth misses the sun.

As the eggcup misses the egg
and an ark misses the flood,
as a knee misses the leg
and veins miss blood.

As a mule misses the horse
and laughter misses mirth,
as a coffin misses its corpse,
as death misses birth.

An Aviary of Small Birds

My love is an aviary
of small birds
and I must learn
to leave the door ajar...

Are you the sparrow
who landed when I sat
at a slate table
sowing lettuces?

Webbs Wonder, Lollo
Rosso, English Cos...
Swift and deft
you flit and peck peck

quick as the light that
constitutes your spirit.
Yes, you were briefer
than Neruda's octobrine.

So much rain that night.
Our room is an ocean
where swallows dive.
The bubble bursts

too soon, too late, too long:
all sorts of microscopia
swim upstream, float in
on summer's storm.

The tenor of your heart
is true as a tuning fork struck
—and high! My love
is the bird who flies free.

Tasting Note for Grief #17

after Do Ho Suh's Staircase 3

Long and complex on the palate
rage attacks the tastebuds,
a territorial robin whose wings
coruscate the epiglottis, insidious
as rust in a cut. Her jaw
has started to clamp. Remembering
is a port wine stain.
        Similes are useless
on this red staircase
that ascends:
an upside down madder root
feeling its way to the sky.
She has become a connoisseur
of its avoided flavours' Titian hues.
The nose has notes of cherry soda,
ginger biscuit, *sang de boeuf.*
This is one for laying down:
it will keep for years under the earth.

The Wish

spreads its branches so twigs scratch
third-floor windows, pushes through cracked
glass into front rooms cluttered with books.

Every time the wish is amended, cells disperse,
subdivide, multiply. Tomorrow the wish is a horse,
a knight with its two forward one across,

his mane a scythe razing cornfields to the ground.
The wish isn't supposed to do that. The wish is out
of control. The wish can be viewed from many angles;

today it's a crow looking for soft spots to stab.
Or a tricolor to wave at the *toros* who charge
with muscled heads down. The wish lives

in a little silver box with WISH written on it.
The wish is big as America. The wish is totally irrelevant.
The wish is yappy as a tethered dog and industrial

in its persistence: a rhesus monkey that bares its teeth.
On anniversaries the wish smiles like a chaise longue;
its death cry sonorous as a foghorn.

The wish is as monumentally unfinished
as Gaudí's dripping *catedral*
and needs you, always, to be absolutely specific.

The wish purrs behind an electrified fence where
it keeps company with deer. The wish is a murmur
barely overheard. The wish. Always the wish.